I0022833

Percy Bysshe Shelley, Harry Buxton Forman

A Proposal

For Putting Reform to the Vote throughout the Kingdom

Percy Bysshe Shelley, Harry Buxton Forman

A Proposal
For Putting Reform to the Vote throughout the Kingdom

ISBN/EAN: 9783744746755

Printed in Europe, USA, Canada, Australia, Japan

Cover: Foto ©Suzi / pixelio.de

More available books at **www.hansebooks.com**

A PROPOSAL

FOR PUTTING REFORM TO THE VOTE

THROUGHOUT THE KINGDOM

BY

THE HERMIT OF MARLOW
[PERCY BYSSHE SHELLEY]

Fac-simile
OF THE
HOLOGRAPH MANUSCRIPT
WITH AN
Introduction by
H BUXTON FORMAN

London
PUBLISHED FOR THE SHELLEY SOCIETY
BY REEVES AND TURNER 196 STRAND
1887

ALBION HOUSE, MARLOW, BUCKS,
SHELLEY'S RESIDENCE IN 1817.

*Fac-simile of a Woodcut published in
" The Mirror of Literature, Amusement,
and Instruction," for Saturday the
2nd of March 1833, No. 593,
Vol. XXI, p. 129.*

The substance of the following Introduction, although intended in the first place for the present purpose, was read at a Meeting of the Shelley Society on the 13th of April 1887, and has also appeared in " The Gentleman's Magazine" for May 1887, in the form of an article entitled " The Hermit of Marlow: a Chapter in the History of Reform."

CONTENTS.

INTRODUCTION

INTRODUCTION.

IN the year 1817 the wretchedness and unrest of the lower classes in England had taken a form sufficiently marked to be the occasion of grave disquietude on the part of the government and the privileged and predatory classes, while, to the liberal-minded and tender-hearted, the need for some alleviation of a general kind for the wide-spread misery and oppression was fast becoming more and more visibly urgent. To make matters worse, the year 1816 had been a bad year for the farmers. There were countless mechanics and labourers who had been thrown out of work in consequence of the introduction of machinery, and the already growing power of foreign nations to compete with us in trade and manufacture. Then, as now, there were plenty of demagogues engaged in stirring

B

up the people to rash action; and then, as *not* now, there were government spies who earned a good living by mixing with the disaffected, inciting them to acts and utterances which could be construed into sedition or treason, and then betraying their poor dupes to the gaol or even the gallows. The people were practically unrepresented in Parliament, and were to a great extent at the mercy of those who had no mercy, the shameful Liverpool administration,—Castlereagh, Sidmouth, Eldon, and Company. Moreover, in the previous year, 1816, the working classes, ignorant though honest in the main, had been sufficiently rash and tumultuous in their agitations for reform to create a strong feeling against them in the great and powerful middle class; and the last complete year which Shelley passed in his own country was marked by a positive decline of the cause of reform. It is true the people had still their staunch and hardy advocates of several kinds and degrees. Major Cartwright and Sir Francis Burdett and the Honourable Douglas Kinnaird were their strong and bold supporters among public men; William Cobbett and William Hone were performing rough literary labour in the popular cause ; Leigh Hunt, whose nature fitted him better for the purlieus of dilettantedom, had thrown himself into the hurley-burley of the same cause, and was doing good work in *The Examiner*; and there was altogether a goodly and growing "cloud of witnesses" for the rights of the people. And yet, when Shelley passed his latest Christmas at an English fire-side, the year was closing in utter blankness as to any public good which had been accomplished. The reform meetings and petitions had for the moment failed ; an attempted interference with the legal robbery carried on by the holding of sinecures had ended in smoke ; and the popular cause was for the moment as a stream returning towards its source. It may possibly have been a perception of this retrograde tendency in the politics of his country that called into fresh and strengthened activity the reforming spirit of Shelley, and goaded him not merely to produce the two essays in concrete politics which mark the year 1817, but also to compose his largest work, that daring *Laon and Cythna* whereby he hoped to awaken the better classes of his countrymen and

countrywomen from their apathy, and startle them into
a moral and intellectual fermentation calculated to bring
about reform in all departments, radical, sweeping, and
conclusive. But I think he can hardly have perceived
the retrogression so early as February, when his reform
pamphlet was probably written, for at that time the
great crusade that was going on in the early part of the
year,—the crusade of the reform meetings held by
influential people, and numberless petitions for reform
addressed to the House of Commons,—had not yet
failed of its object. I think he must have been urged to
issue this particular pamphlet by a wise perception that
some of the most prominent reformers were asking not
only what it was next to impossible to grant, but what
the people were not ripe to exercise—universal suffrage.
It was certainly not that he had nothing particular to
do just then, no urgent personal cares to occupy him, no
members of his own more intimate circle claiming help and
active sympathy, no dreadful memories of recent events
to harass him, and no impending disasters to struggle
against. On the contrary, the year 1816 had not only
seen the death of Harriett Shelley and Fanny Godwin

by suicide, incidents unspeakably harrowing to him,—
not only did the close of that year witness the beginning
of his troubles about Harriett's children ; but the fiery
planet Byron had come into the Shelleyan sphere and
left him with the charge of Claire Clairmont, about to
become the mother of Allegra Byron ; while Godwin,
Leigh Hunt, and Peacock, with their "large claims of
general justice," were never far off.

During the first two months of 1817 Shelley was
greatly occupied with preparations for the Chancery
suit, which eventually deprived him definitely of the
charge of Ianthe and Charles ; and in January Claire's
little Allegra was born at Bath, Mary Shelley being also
there, and Shelley in London.   Shortly Mary joined
him in London ; and it was seemingly during the busy
time immediately preceding their settlement at Marlow
that the political situation appeared to him so pressing as
to call forth *A Proposal for Putting Reform to the Vote
throughout the Kingdom* : it was apparently while the
Chancery suit was still pending ; for the pamphlet came
out about the middle of March, and Lord Eldon's
decision on the suit was not given till the 27th.

C

The house which Shelley had taken at Marlow, to occupy "for ever" with Mary and her child, if not with Claire and the little Allegra and many regular or desultory camp-followers, bore the propitious name of "Albion House." The household migrated to Marlow "in the last week in February," says Professor Dowden,[1] "before the house was ready." Shelley was back in London before taking possession, and finally "seems to have entered the house in the week March 9—16."[2] This perpetual residence was secured, it seems, just in time to yield a pseudonym for the poet, who was then suffering keenly from the baleful effects of two early works filed by the Westbrooks in the Court of Chancery, in support of allegations made to deprive him of the custody of his children. The fact that *Queen Mab* and the *Letter to Lord Ellenborough* had been used against him, though with results not then disclosed, may have influenced him to conceal his authorship of the reform pamphlet; for, though moderate compared with much writing of the period on the Liberal side, the *Proposal* was still sufficiently daring, and would, in the eyes of Lord Eldón, the

[1] *Life of Shelley*, vol. ii, p. 110.   [2] *Ibid.*

Westbrooks, and other magnates and nobodies, have added to his religious and social enormities a definite attempt at political agitation. For whatever reason, he elected to place upon the pamphlet no author's name, and to let it go out to the world as from " The Hermit of Marlow,"—a designation which it pleased him to keep during the greater part of his residence in that primitive Buckinghamshire town on the banks of the Thames, though it must be confessed that "Albion House," albeit not then cut up into tenements and turned in part into a public-house as it is now, was not in any respect like a hermitage. It stood, as it stands to-day, right on the roadside (West Street is the name of the road ; but it is still not much like a street) ; and solitude was not a marked characteristic of the conditions of residence at Marlow. Whether Shelley's friends knew him in 1817 as " The Hermit," I cannot say ; but he himself brought out the title for use again in November, when he issued his second political pamphlet of 1817, ostensibly *An Address to the People on the Death of the Princess Charlotte*, but really an eloquent appeal against the iniquitous execution of Brandreth,

Turner, and Ludlam, the victims of the government spy
Oliver and one of those bogus conspiracies which were
an ugly feature of the anti-popular tactics in those days
of " Murder, Fraud, and Anarchy."

But to return to the Hermit's first Marlow pamphlet,
the manuscript of which (first and last manuscript, I
should judge), now in the possession of Mr. Thomas J.
Wise, is reproduced in the following pages. The same
good fortune which, as we shall see anon, attended the
scheme of reform advocated in the pamphlet, attended
also the tangible substance incorporating that scheme,—
that is to say if preservation is to be regarded as a
desideratum. Unlike the Hermit's other pamphlet, of
which no manuscript, or proof-sheet, or copy of the
original issue is known to be extant, the *Proposal* is preserved in all three stages. Not only have copies of the
extremely rare print come down to us, but the proof-
sheets revised by Shelley, and bearing sketchy drawings
from his pen, were preserved by Leigh Hunt, and are
now in the collection of Sir Percy and Lady Shelley ;
while the original manuscript, roughly and rapidly
written, and full of erasures and corrections, remained in

the hands of Mr. Ollier, the publisher, whose family, in
the fulness of time, sold it. This took place in July
1877 ; and I refrain now from any textual examination
of the manuscript, because Mr. Francis Harvey of St.
James's Street, who bought this holograph at auction in
the ordinary way of business, gave me, with exemplary
courtesy and generosity, full opportunity to exhaust the
subject when I reprinted the pamphlet in my edition of
Shelley's *Prose Works* (4 volumes, 1880). I believe the
foot-notes to the *Proposal* give all that can be given in
the way of variorum readings and cancelled passages ;
and it is a pleasure to me to think that Mr. Harvey, of
whom I had no previous knowledge, and on whom I ·
certainly had no claim, entertained an angel unawares.
Not that I was the angel ; but it was the record of the
particulars of the manuscript in my notes that eventually
found Mr. Harvey a customer for his costly treasure in
the person of Mr. Wise.

But the luck of preservation connected with the *Proposal* goes further yet. As far as I know there is but one
reference to the Princess Charlotte pamphlet in all the
extant Shelley correspondence. Mrs. Shelley's diary

records that he began a pamphlet on the 11th of November and finished it on the 12th; and there is a little note to Ollier, dated the 12th, sending a part of the manuscript for press.[1] These are doubtless references to the *Address*; but in the case of the *Proposal* we have Shelley's instructions to his publisher in some detail. The following letter is undated, un-post-marked, and, I believe, unpublished :—

DEAR SIR,

I inclose you the Revise which may be put to press when corrected, and the sooner the better. I inclose you also a list of persons to whom I wish copies to be sent *from the Author*, as soon as possible. I trust you will be good enough to take the trouble off my hands.—

Do not advertise sparingly: and get as many book-sellers as you can to take copies on their own account. Sherwood Neely & Co, Hone of Newgate Street, Ridgeway, and Stockdale are people likely to do so —Send 20 or 30 copies to Messrs. Hookham & Co Bond Street without explanation. I have arranged with them.

Send 20 copies to me addressed to Mr. Hunt, who will know what to do with them if I am out of town.—

Your very obedient Ser^t

P. B. SHELLEY

[1] Dowden's *Life of Shelley*, vol. ii, p. 158.

The list which Shelley sent to Mr. Ollier in the foregoing letter was a pretty considerable one, designed to
dispose of fifty-seven copies of the pamphlet, besides the
forty or fifty referred to in the letter; and the instructions
as to advertizing and so on indicate regular publication.
According to entries made on the list, thirty-one copies
were sent out " from the Author." A copy also appears
to have reached either Southey or *The Quarterly Review*;
for in the heading to his article on " The Rise and Progress of Popular Disaffection,"[1] the title of Shelley's pamphlet figures, though the *Proposal* is not alluded to in the
text of the article. On the whole the pamphlet ought
not to be so extremely rare; and the Shelley Society
will probably stir up hiding-holes and bring copies
to light.

In another extant letter to Mr. Ollier, written at
Marlow on the 14th of March 1817, the Hermit asks
" How does the pamphlet sell?" Of the answer we know
nothing; but it was probably the negative to which he was
already well accustomed; and in this case the incongruity
between the bold title and the shy retiring pseudonym

[1] *Quarterly* for January 1817, published the following April.

might not unnaturally have deterred from purchase even
the very elect of reformers.

When one wants to form an idea of the influences
working from without, at a particular time, on a man
vitally interested as Shelley was in the progress of
public affairs, it is no bad plan, leisure permitting, to
consult a file of some contemporary daily newspaper
and the relative volumes of Hansard's *Parliamentary
Debates.* In default of leisure or opportunity for bring-
ing this cumbrous apparatus to bear on the present
subject, I will turn over the leaves of a weekly newspaper of 1817 instead ; and how can I do better than
take Leigh Hunt's ultra-radical print, *The Examiner,*
with its audacious "Leontian" leaders, its excellent
parliamentary and other reports, and its varied and
multitudinous notes of news ? Moreover, this paper
for 1817 is not unembellished by the genius of many
of the Shelley circle ; and it is a pleasure to glance
over pages in which we are conscious of the presence
of Leigh Hunt *passim,* stumble upon sonnets by
Keats, meet once and again Haydon and Hazlitt,
fall in with dear delightful Horace Smith, and even

get a taste of the quality of Shelley himself, who was a contributor of Hunt's as well as a constant reader.

Before we take to our *Examiner*, it will be worth while to glance down that list of persons to whom Shelley ordered his publishers to send the *Proposal for Putting Reform to the Vote*. This list I printed in *The Shelley Library*, Part I, page 67; but I reprint it now, for convenience of reference, in the Appendix to these remarks. In it we read the names of most of the persons marked by liberal views on whose track we shall presently come in our radical newspaper.

The year opens propitiously for us; for on New Year's Day the patriarchal reformer Major Cartwright took the chair at a meeting of the Westminster Electors at the Crown and Anchor, convened to receive from their popular and gallant representative in Parliament, Lord Cochrane, his answer to an address which they had voted him in assurance of their continued confidence and admiration. Lord Cochrane's manly reply alludes to the support and protection he has had from liberal Westminster during three years of persecution

E

for those well-known attacks on naval abuses to which
his position in the navy had given the sting of truth.
" After many strong and interesting statements, he
recommended to the Meeting to continue to support
Parlimentary Reform, for without it the people of
England would remain oppressed, persecuted, enslaved,
and starving." In the course of the proceedings a
Mr. Wells was hissed for proposing so weak a measure
of reform as triennial parliaments : he explained that
he really wanted annual ones, but thought "if that
object could not be obtained, it were better to go step
by step until they could obtain it." A Mr. Walker[1]
having remarked that he "was for arriving at the
wished-for object at once," the redoubted Major
delivered his conviction that triennial parliaments
could not be beneficial if obtained. He mentioned
as evidence of the exertions then being made that he
had five hundred petitions in his house to present at
the meeting of Partiament, and had issued three hundred
more forms to be filled up : he named 2,400 as the
total number of petitions likely to be presented ; and he

[1] See Shelley's list.

concluded by emphatically stating that annual representation was the only cure for existing evils.

Five days later, for anything I can hear to the contrary, Shelley may have attended a huge meeting at Bath. Claire was certainly in that city; and Shelley and Mary had secured places in the coach, for the 1st of January, to join her: it was still early in January when he left the two ladies at Bath, to return to London on his Chancery business; and if, as I think, he was at Bath on the 6th, he would hardly have missed the occasion to attend a meeting of upwards of 6,000 people to petition Parliament for a redress of grievances and particularly for parliamentary reform. On this momentous occasion "large bodies of military, both horse and foot, were in readiness in case of a riot; and most of the principal inhabitants were sworn in special constables on the occasion," when "Orator" Hunt was "to the fore," and made a long speech in his usual rough and ready, pugnacious style, specially condemning the attempt of the authorities to intimidate the assembly. Turning the page again, we find our *Examiner* recording that four sailors, on the day after this meeting, were hung for stealing ships; and here was another call for reform which must have seemed desperately urgent to our tender-hearted and tolerant poet.

To *The Examiner* for the 19th of January he contributed his *Hymn to Intellectual Beauty*, of which, by the bye, I am pretty sure he must have revised a proof; and immediately after his signature comes the word REFORM at the head of a report of a "Select Meeting of Independent Gentlemen, friends of economy, public order, and reform,"—which had been held on the 17th of January. The most prominent names on this occasion are those of Curran, Alderman Waithman, and Alderman Goodbehere, names which are all in Shelley's list referred to above. Curran made a capital speech, wherein he remarked that parliamentary reform did not "consist in breaking windows or getting drunk in the streets,"—a remark not wholly inapplicable to some of the so-called reformers of our own day.

The report of this meeting is followed by one of a meeting held at Dublin on the previous Monday, the

13th of January, under the eye, as one of the speakers (O'Connell) observed, "of ten regiments of soldiers under arms, and two troops of artillery ready for immediate action." This meeting, described as "a vast concourse of people," dispersed and "returned in the greatest order to their homes," after passing several resolutions, and agreeing to a petition, which I give in the Appendix as a representative document whose terms must have been familiar to Shelley.

The day after this meeting, a boy who bore the suggestive patronymic of Dogood was sent to prison in London for tearing down some bills posted in Long Acre, headed "Mr. Hunt hissed out of Bristol." The animus of the authorities against the "Orator" and the cause he represented is obvious.

On the 22nd of January another reform meeting took place at the Crown and Anchor,—William Cobbett, Henry Hunt, and Major Cartwright being the most prominent speakers. Mr. Jones Burdett [1] brought word from the London Hampden Club that he and Major Cartwright were deputed by that Club to lay before

---

[1] See Shelley's list in Appendix.

F

the Reform Delegates assembled at the meeting the heads of a bill to be submitted to Parliament. The material principles recognized by this bill were (1) household suffrage, (2) division of counties and cities into electoral districts, each returning one member, according to population, and (3) annual elections. Major Cartwright said that, though in favour of universal suffrage, he must admit that many "sound reformists entertained other opinions on the ground of practicability." Cobbett spoke most contemptuously of the Club, but excepted from his denunciation Sir Francis Burdett, Mr. Jones Burdett, Major Cartwright, and "that sound patriot Mr. Hallet of Berks." [1] Henry Hunt, while endorsing Cobbett's contemptuous view of the Club, managed to carry, against him, a resolution in favour of "representation co-existent with taxation." A skirmish between the "Orator" and the reporters of *The Morning Chronicle* and *The British Press* gave variety to the proceedings:

[1] Note that this same gentleman, "Mr. Hallet of Berkshire," was to receive five copies according to Shelley's list, and the London Hampden Club ten. I suppose Berkshire was not a sufficiently definite address for Ollier, no copies having apparently been sent to Mr. Hallet.

Hunt, always in hot water, accused the daily press of systematic misrepresentation of reform meetings ; and the two reporters resented the insult and denied the charge.

One day later (23 January 1817) Alderman Good-behere and Alderman Waithman [1] took a prominent . part in a reform meeting of the Common Council, at which the resolutions were so significant that I give them in the Appendix.

Turning to other parts of our *Examiner* for the 26th of January, we come on some occult allusions of Leigh Hunt's to Shelley's Chancery case, and on an inaccurate little report, taken from *The Morning Chronicle*, of the proceedings on Friday the 24th of January in the matter of Westbrook *v.* Shelley. " His Lordship is to give judgment on a future day," says the report. On the same page begins the report of the trial of a sailor named Cashman and others in the matter of the musket-stealing connected with the riots of two months earlier. Cashman was found guilty and condemned to death.

On the 28th of January the Prince Regent opened

[1] See Shelley's list.

Parliament: on his way back to the palace he got
hooted and pelted; and the windows of his carriage were
broken. On the following Sunday *The Examiner* was of
course full of the attack and the opening of Parliament.
On the 29th Lord Cochrane began the reform petition
campaign by presenting a petition from Bristol signed
by over 50,000 people ; and, after a full parliamentary
report, we find in *The Examiner* for the 2nd of February
in an appropriate setting of reform paragraphs, an
editorial correction of inaccuracies in the report of
Westbrook *v.* Shelley, immediately followed by Horace
Smith's sonnet, commencing with the line

"Eternal and Omnipotent Unseen!"

Shelley's battle to regain possession of his children was
of course regarded in his immediate circle not only as
a personal question of desperate interest, but as an
important issue in the general question of fundamental
reform. The issue was indeed momentous—being no
less than a dispute as to the right of a father, of
what opinions soever in religious, moral, and social
questions, to control and educate his own children. Note

that in this, as in most of the reform battles fought in the reign of Eldon, Castlereagh, Sidmouth and Co., the popular party, the party of freedom and equal laws, failed grievously and utterly.

But we must keep to our *Examiner* a little longer.

On the 3rd of February, as reported in the paper of the 9th, the reform petitions to Parliament were varied by one from the boy Dogood, who had been sent to prison for tearing down scurrilous posters about "Orator" Hunt. That petition was rejected ; and the boy was referred to the Law Courts.

Sir Francis Burdett and Lord Cochrane now appear in constant collision with Lord Castlereagh, Mr. Vansittart, or some one else of the kind,—every petition brought forward being subjected to obstruction, and Brougham [1] frequently rising to put in a pregnant word for the petitioners.

The Examiner of the 10th of January has the agreeable variety of a sonnet from Keats, that to Kosciusko, flanked by reports of Henry Hunt's vulgarity at a reform meeting and of a discreditable fracas between

---

[1] See Shelley's list.

him and Morley the hotel keeper. Perhaps this blunder-
ing coarseness, which was characteristic enough of the
"Orator," prevented Shelley from sending him the pamphlet : at all events his name is conspicuous for its
absence from the list, though two years later, *àpropos*
of "Peterloo," Shelley commended his conduct. The
same day's paper has a report of a meeting in Palace
Yard, Westminster, on the 13th of February, to vote an
address of the inhabitants of Westminster to the Regent
concerning the attack on his carriage. As usual, Sir
Francis Burdett, Major Cartwright, Lord Cochrane, and
Henry Hunt were in the van. The address voted was a
clever, sarcastic document, really, with mock humility,
making light of the attack, and inculcating on his
royal highness the urgent need for reform.

From *The Examiner* for the 23rd of February we gather
in passing that, at that time, seventy-three men and fifteen
women were lying under sentence of death in Newgate
gaol. Mr. Bennet [1] used this fact for an indirect attack

---

[1] The only M.P. of the name that I can trace in 1817 is the Hon.
H. G. Bennet. Shelley's list includes Captain Bennet, M.P., to whom a
copy of the pamphlet seems to have been sent.

on Lord Eldon ; and Lord Castlereagh " deemed the Hon. gentleman's speech very inflammatory, and directed against high legal officers. The delay," he said, "did not rest with the Chancellor." Mr. Bennet's object seems to have been to force the Chancellor and the Secretary of State to prepare a list of these wretched people for the Prince Regent, with a view of getting their miseries abridged either one way or another. It appears there was hope that the majority would not really suffer the penalty of death. Turning from this disgraceful business to another page of the paper, we find relief (and let us hope Shelley did) in Keats's sonnet

" After dark vapors have oppress'd our plains " . . .

One more leaf turned, and we meet " Orator " Hunt in the Court of King's Bench before Shelley's old bugbear Lord Ellenborough, urging, but without any satisfactory result, the case of the boy Dogood, whom Parliament had referred to the Law Courts.

The accounts of reform meetings, and of the proceedings in Parliament about the petitions occupy a great deal

of space in *The Examiner.* We know that Shelley was a
regular reader of the paper ; and the chances are that
he read every word of what we have been glancing at,
and a vast deal more on these subjects. The petition
phenomenon seems to have struck Mrs. Shelley ; for, in
a letter to Leigh Hunt inviting him to Marlow, she says,
"You shall never be serious when you wish to be
merry, and have as many nuts to crack as there are
words in the Petitions to Parliament for Reform—a
tremendous promise." [1]

Now Shelley's small contribution to this reform agitation is a really practical and not impracticable one.
Seeing how the contest raged in Parliament, how little
real impression on that corrupt chamber and insolently
unprincipled administration was being produced by the
fiery onslaughts of Sir Francis Burdett, the frank and
gallant pertinacity of Lord Cochrane, the logical incisive-
ness of Henry Brougham, the cool, consistent, decisive
hammering of Major Cartwright, at the close of his forty
years' experience in popular agitation ; seeing behind the
parliamentary spectacle the great surging ocean of misery

[1] Dowden's *Life of Shelley,* vol. ii, p. 112.

and agitation; and hearing the repeated question, "*Is*
parliamentary reform the will of the people,"—he said
"Let us see." How? By taking the sense of the people.
The object of Shelley's pamphlet was to hold a meeting in order to organize a deliberate *plébiscite*, and to
abide by the result. If reform should prove to be the
will of the majority, Parliament must grant it or be
deemed in rebellion against the people. If only a
minority demanded reform, it would rest with them to go
on petitioning till they attained their end by attraction
and accretion.

. Not only was this proposal for a meeting at the Crown
and Anchor tavern a reasonable and practicable one;
but the Hermit was ready to give a tenth of his year's
income towards the expenses of the *plébiscite*. Moreover, he expressed surprisingly moderate views. Major
Cartwright's position as to universal suffrage he admitted
to be logically impregnable; but he also pointed out
that, logically, the preëminent advantages of a republic
could not be disputed. He did not think England
ripe either for republican government or for universal
suffrage, because the men of the lowest class had been

H

rendered "brutal and torpid and ferocious by ages of slavery." He therefore thought that "none but those who register their names as paying a certain small sum in *direct taxes* ought, at present, to send members to Parliament." As to annual elections, he endorsed unhesitatingly the views of Cartwright and Cobbett.

In the long run, Shelley's reputation had the advantage proper to the moderate and sagacious tone of this pamphlet ; for, as Mr. Rossetti says,[1] "The whirligig of time has brought-in many revenges to Shelley, and this amongst others—that the Tories found it their interest and necessity to pass in 1867 almost the very scheme of Reform which the poet and ' dreamer,' the atheist and democrat, had suggested in 1817 ; for it makes little difference whether we speak of a payment of money in

[1] *A Memoir of Shelley (with a Fresh Preface)*, Shelley Society, 1886, p. 80. Note another of Time's revenges : a great poet in 1817 advocates a scheme of reform carried out by the Conservatives in 1867 ; and then an admirable poet still among us characterizes the year, the men, and the deed thus :—

" In the Year of the great Crime,
  When the false English nobles and their Jew,
  By God demented, slew
  The Trust they stood thrice pledged to keep from wrong, . . .'
                          (*Odes*, by COVENTRY PATMORE, 1868.)

'direct taxes' or in 'rating.' " Meanwhile, the leading
ideas of that gallant Major whom Shelley regarded as
unanswerable, and who was one of the most influential
politicians of his land and day, await fulfilment. Indeed,
although the rushing wheels of our civilizing machine
are fast driving out of any living place in our memory
men whose work, like that of Cartwright and Burdett, is
not of a form and visible substance to command in-
tegral preservation, I cannot leave John Cartwright
without a few more words.

It is difficult for us to realize at the present day the
importance of the position which he occupied in 1817,
as well as earlier and later. When Shelley wrote his
Proposal, the mere reference to Major Cartwright was
sufficient to carry with it four clear and very advanced
ideas, to wit, universal suffrage, equal representation,
vote by ballot, and annual parliaments : it was as the
" firm, consistent, and persevering advocate " of those
principles that he was described at the base of a statue
of him erected in Burton Crescent just before the
Reform Bill of 1832 was passed. This was under
the administration of Earl Grey, who was an old

adherent to the principles of Major Cartwright, however much it may have been found expedient to water down those principles in the work of 1832, so as to give the power to the middle class and not to the people. This "firm, consistent, and persevering advocate" of righteous views, whereof some yet await fulfilment, had been a genuine force in England : born far back in the eighteenth century,[1] his eventful and philanthropic life was drawing to its close when Shelley became convinced of the need to retrench those magnificent schemes of reform. Cartwright's *Reasons for Reformation* (1809) and *The Comparison, in which Mock Reform, Half Reform, and Constitutional Reform, are considered* (1810), familiar far and wide in 1817, succeeded a long array of political pamphlets, treatises, &c. ; and Shelley would doubtless have thought it as impertinent as it was unnecessary to particularize the views and arguments to which he alludes in *A Proposal*

[1] Born 1740—died 1824 : he was brother, by the bye, to that Edmund Cartwright who invented the power-loom ; and another brother, George, was the intrepid navigator who made six voyages to the coast of Labrador, passed in all nearly sixteen years there, and published in 1793, in three quarto volumes, a *Journal of Transactions and Events* during that long residence in an inhospitable country.

for Putting Reform to the Vote. That *Proposal*, good as it is, was a poor little tract compared with Cartwright's achievements; but we must take the world as we find it; and, while the splendour of Shelley's intellectual and literary gifts makes it natural for us to attempt to gather, investigate, and illustrate all he ever did, the true, honest men who only worked hard for the enfranchisement of their less fortunate fellow men, only gave their lives, their hearts, their heads, and their energies, must be deemed fortunate if allowed even to sit on the lowest steps of the temple of fame, while the upper steps are reserved for the men of genius who are already beginning to be crowded and jostled out of the inner sanctum.

H. BUXTON FORMAN.

46, MARLBOROUGH HILL, ST. JOHN'S WOOD,
March, 1887.

I

APPENDIX

APPENDIX.

I.

The " Free List" for Shelley's "Proposal for Putting Reform to the Vote."

Sir Francis Burdett M.P.*
Mr. Peters of Cornwall
Mr. Brougham M.P.*
Lord Grosvenor *
Lord Holland *
Lord Grey *
Mr. Cobbett *
Mr. Waithman *
Mr. Curran
Hon. Douglas Kinnaird *
Hon. Thos. Brand M.P.*
Lord Cochrane M.P.
Sir R. Heron M.P.
The Lord Mayor *
Mr. Montague Burgoyne
Major Cartwright *
Messrs. Taylor Sen. & Jun. of Norwich
Mr. Place, Charing Cross *
Mr. Walker of Westminster
Lord Essex *
Capt. Bennet M.P.*
The Birmingham Hampden Club (5 copies)

Mr. I. Thomas, St. Albans, Mon.
Mr. Philipps, Whitston, Mon.
Mr. Andrew Duncan, Provost of Arbroath
Mr. Alderman Goodbehere *
Mr. Jones Burdett *
Mr. Hallet of Berkshire (5 copies)
.The London Hampden Club (10 copies) *
The Editors of the Statesman * the Morning Chronicle * and the Independent Whig *
Mr. Montgomery (the Poet) of Sheffield
Mr. R. Oven of Lanark
Mr. Madocks M.P.
Mr. George Ensor
Mr. Bruce
Mr. Sturch (of Westminster) *
Mr. Creery M.P.
Gen!. Sir R. Ferguson M.P.*

---

* Against the names distinguished by asterisks the word *sent* was written in the original list, and not by Shelley. I presume this was done at Messrs. Ollier's office, and that copies were really sent to the persons thus indicated.

K

II

Petition [1] *for Reform adopted at a Meeting held in Dublin on the 13th of January* 1817.

PETITION.

Sheweth—That your Petitioners have a full and immoveable conviction, a conviction which they believe to be universal, that your Honourable House doth not, in any constitutional or rational sense, Represent the Nation.

That, when the People have ceased to be Represented, the Constitution is subverted.

That Taxation without Representation is a state of Slavery.

That there is no property in that which any person or persons, any power or authority, can take from the People without their consent.

That your Petitioners hold it to be self-evident, that there are not any human means of redressing the People's wrongs, or composing their distracted minds, or of preventing the subversion of liberty and the establishment of despotism, unless by calling the collective wisdom and virtue of the community into Council by the Election of a free Parliament.

That your Petitioners have peculiar reasons to deplore the substitution of the system of corrupt usurpation of popular rights, in place of the genuine Representation of the People; inasmuch as one of the consequences of that system has inflicted on the great body of your Petitioners, particularly the Manufacturing and Labouring Classes, *by the measure of the Legislative Union,* the permanent existence of Poverty and Distress.

---

[1] The text of the petition is taken from *The Examiner* for the 19th of January 1817.

Wherefore your Petitioners pray, that your Honourable House will, without delay, pass a Bill for putting the aggrieved and much-wronged People in possession of their undoubted rights to Representation, co-extensive with direct and indirect Taxation ; to an equal distribution throughout the community of such Representation ; and to Parliament of a continuance according to the strict letter of the Constitution, namely, *not exceeding one year.*

III.

Resolutions[1] *passed at a Meeting of the Common Council of London on the 23rd of January* 1817.

Resolved—That this Court, at a crisis of such general and unexampled pressure and calamity, feel themselves called upon to lay before Parliament a faithful representation of their grievances.

Resolved—That these grievances, so deeply affecting all classes of Society, are not of a temporary, unforeseen, or unavoidable nature, but are to be traced to a long and fatal course of wanton and wasteful extravagance in the expenditure of the Public Money —to a profusion of useless Places, Sinecures, and unmerited Pensions—to an enormous and unnecessary Standing Army in time of Peace—and to the want of that vigilance and constitutional controul over the Executive Government, which can only spring from a free, equal, and pure Representation of the People in Parliament.

[1] The text of the Resolutions is given from *The Examiner* for the 26th of January 1817.

Resolved—That this Court feel it unnecessary to enter into the afflicting details of Distress and Suffering so universally felt, because they have become too manifest to have escaped the observance of Parliament—the decayed state of Trade—of the Manufactures—of the Agriculture of the Country—with the great depreciation in the value of Property, and the enormous and vexatious weight of Taxation, have grievously affected the inhabitants of the United Kingdom, particularly the middle and laborious classes, and a large portion of the population are compelled to seek subsistence upon charity, or to take refuge in a workhouse.

Resolved—That the present complicated and alarming evils demand immediate and effectual remedy—that, as they have chiefly arisen from the corrupt and inadequate state of the Representation, all attempts to provide an effectual remedy, without a complete and comprehensive Reform in the Commons House of Parliament, would prove delusive, and could neither allay the irritated feelings of the People, or afford security against future encroachments.

Resolved—That we conceive the inequality in the Representation is too notorious to require to be pointed out, when it is known that Cornwall alone returns more Borough Members than 15 other Counties together, including Middlesex, and more than 11 Counties, even including County Members.

Resolved—That the mode of Election, the Influence and Patronage, the distribution of Places and Pensions among the Members and their Relatives, are facts that cannot but be equally well known: and, even in prosperous times, would afford sufficient motive to every friend of freedom and lover of the Constitution to seek for reformation: but, under the present accumulation of distress, which this system has so unhappily engendered and matured, we conceive the motives are become too powerful, too imperious, any longer to be resisted or delayed.

Resolved—That as Extravagance and Corruption in Governments have been the destruction of all free States, so is it impossible that a system, which has proved fatal to other States, should
be innocently pursued in this. We trust, therefore, that there
may be at least one exception to the remark of the Historian,
who has so well described the rise and fall of other Empires,
" *That Individuals sometimes profit by experience—Governments*
NEVER "—and that, by timely reformation, the ruin of the British
Constitution may be averted.

Resolved—That this Court, knowing the misrepresentations
and calumnies that are at all times thrown upon those who are
seeking, in a peaceable and constitutional manner, a redress of
grievances, declare, that we entertain no projects inconsistent
with sound practice and experience. It is to the restoration of
the British Constitution—to the drawing of it back to its true
principles that we look—the shortening the duration of Parliaments, and a fair and equal distribution of the elective franchise
among all Freeholders, Copyholders, and Householders paying
taxes—with such regulations as will preserve the purity and
integrity of the Members, and render the House of Commons
an efficient organ of the People.

Resolved—That for the attainment of these great and national
objects, by effecting a general union and co-operation, and giving
to the national feeling a firm, temperate, peaceable, and constitutional direction, it is become no less the duty than interest of
all persons of rank, character, and property, to give their cordial
and zealous assistance to the people at large ; and we do hereby
invite them thereto, as the best means of promoting and securing
the peace, liberty, happiness, and prosperity of the British Empire.

Resolved—That Petitions, therefore, be presented to Parliament,
praying them to take these matters into their serious consideration, and that they will be pleased immediately to take the most
effective measures for abolishing all Sinecures and unmerited
Pensions—for reducing the present enormous Military Establish-

L

ment—for establishing a general System of Retrenchment and Economy—and for the more effectually obtaining a Redress of all Grievances, and guarding against future Evils, they will cause such a Reform in the Commons House of Parliament as will restore to the People their just and fair weight in the Legislature.

FAC-SIMILE OF SHELLEY'S MANUSCRIPT

A Proposal

~~for a General meeting of the~~

for putting Reform to the Vote
throughout the Kingdom

by The Hermit of Marlow

London

Printed for C & J Ollier
Welbeck St Cavendish Sqr
1817

An Address
to the Reformers

A great question is now agitating in this nation, ~~which~~
which no man or no party of men is competent to decide, ~~or~~
~~to force~~ ~~I think~~ ~~the manner of the~~ the issue in of which
there are no materials of evidence which can afford a foresight of the result.
~~no one is able to predict.~~ ~~the~~ the issue depends whether
we are to be slaves or freemen. ~~God or the its~~

It is needless to recapitulate all that has been said about reform.
Every one is agreed that the House of Commons is not a
representative of the people. The only theoretical question that
remains, is whether the people ought to ~~be assemble or not~~
legislate for themselves, or be governed by laws assented
~~which & in provisions~~ by taxes originating in the edicts
~~of such less~~ in assembly which represents somewhat
less than a thousandth part of the entire community.
I think they ought not to be so taxed ~~&~~

hospital for lunatics is the only scene where we can con
ever so mournful to conceive to be exhibited as this
mighty nation now exhibits: ~~as that~~ a single person
betraying & swindling a thousand of his comrades ~~out of~~
all they possessed in the world, & then trampling &

spit upon them, tho' he were the most contemptible &
degraded of mankind, if they had strength in their
arms & courage in their hearts. ~~to us~~ such a
resolve realised in political society is a spectacle
worthy of the utmost indignation & abhorrence. —

The prerogative of Parliament ~~have been increased~~
~~is contempt~~ constitute a sovereignty which ~~has been~~
exercised in contempt of the people, & it is in ~~their~~
~~broken consist~~ that I consistency with the laws of
human nature, that it sh'd have been exercised
for the people's misery & ruin. Those whom they
despise, men instinctively seek to render slavish
& wretched that their scorn may be secure. It is
~~the object of~~ It is the object of the Reformers to
restore the people to ~~their~~ ~~sovereignty which has been usurped~~
~~a sovereignty that has in their contempt~~
~~excite them to possess them sense of their rights~~. It
is my object, or I would be silent now.

Servitude is sometimes voluntary. Perhaps
the people choose to be enslaved, perhaps it is their
will to be degraded & ignorant & famished ~~wretched~~
fanaticism of custom ~~had so securely wooed them~~
~~to its enchantments so securely that they~~

would rather /~~fight with~~ ~~their wives & their children~~
see their /wives & children starve by inches ~~there dare~~
rather heat & ~~of~~ without ingratiation all the ~~continuecies~~
~~of the~~ ~~persecution the powerful~~, rather ~~work sixteen hours~~
a day. Perhaps custom is their only God, & they
its fanatic worshippers, ~~or they~~ will shiver in front
& waste in famine rather than deny that Idol.
Perhaps the majority of this nation decree that
they ~~shall~~ ~~live in squalidness~~ want, ~~that they~~
~~shall not~~ not be represented in Parliament, that
they will not to deprive of ~~their~~ power those who
have seduced them to the miserable condition ~~of~~
~~begging the~~ in which they now exist. ~~Is such~~
~~If such be~~ It is their will — it is their own concern.
If such be their decision, the champions of the
rights of & the mourners over the errors & calamities
of men, must return to their homes in silence, until
~~suffering~~ accumulated sufferings shall have produced the
effect of reason:—

The question now at issue, is whether the majority
of the adult individuals of the United Kingdom of
Great Britain & Ireland, ~~a complete desire~~ or ~~no~~
a complete representation in the legislature

Assemblies.

~~If that question is answered in the affirmative~~
I have no doubt that such is their ~~desire~~ will, &
~~that this such is~~ I believe this ~~opinion private~~
opinion of most persons conversant with the
state of public feeling. But ~~is ought~~ the
fact ought to be formally ascertained before
we proceed. ~~If the reformers are really in the~~
If the majority of the adult population
~~shall~~ should & solemnly state their desire to be, that
~~they should be adequately represented~~ the representatives
whom they might appoint should constitute the
common house of Parliament ~~if~~ there is an
end of the dispute. Parliament would then be
required, not petitioned to prepare some effectual
plan ~~for carrying same of will into effect~~ And if Parliament should
then refuse — the consequences of the contest
that ~~would~~ ensue, would not in ~~their~~ its presumption
& temerity be alone Parliament would have whether
against the people ~~French~~
If the majority of the adult population

shall, when seriously called upon for their opinion, so
determine, on grounds however momentous, that the
experiment of innovation by reform in Parliament is an
evil of greater magnitude than the consequences
of misgovernment which to which we all this to which
afford a constitutional
sanction... then it becomes us to be silent. — &
we should be guilty of the a great crime
which I have conditionally imputed to
the House of Commons, if after the foregoing
virtual expression of the general will, that to
acquiesced in the existing system we should,
by partial assemblies of the people or multitude
or by any party act excite the minority to
distrust this decision. — Let the

Let this paint to the first step
towards reform us to ascertain this point

~~Senate~~

For ~~this~~ purpose I think the following plan ~~would~~ be effectual.

~~To call a meeting~~ That you, sir, should ~~call a meeting to be held~~ That a meeting should be appointed to be held at the Crown & Anchor Tavern on the seventeenth of March, ~~& that all the~~ ~~friends of reform be~~ ~~at~~ invited to attend that meeting. ~~for the purchase of~~ to lapse into consideration the most effectual measures for ascertaining whether or no, a Reform in Parliament ~~was~~ is the will of the majority of the individuals of the ~~British Nation.~~

~~That the friends of reform be now residing~~ ~~in any part of the country should be recom~~ ~~the intimate to be present at this meeting.~~

That ~~all the~~ friends the most eloquent & the most virtuous & the most venerable among you should employ all your authority & interest to persuade men to lay aside

all discussion respecting the topics on which they
are disunited, & by the love which they bear
to their suffering country conjure them to concentrate
all their energies to set this great question
at rest — whether the nation obtain a reform in
Parliament or no.

That the friends of Reform residing in any
part of the country be earnestly
intreated to lend perhaps their last
& the decisive effort to set their hopes & fears
at rest. — that those who can, should come
to London, & those who cannot
but who yet feel that the aid of their fraternity
might be beneficial should address a letter to
the chairman of the meeting explaining their
sentiments. Let these letters be read aloud, let
all things be transacted in the face of day.

Let Resolutions of an import similar to those
that follow be proposed.

1. ~~That the Reformers deny the imputation to~~
~~That those~~ who think that is the duty of the
People of this Nation to exact a ~~full representation~~
such a reform in the Common House of Parliament,
as should make that House a ~~full~~ a complete
representation of their will, & ~~that~~ the People
have a right to perform this duty, ~~are now~~
~~have~~ assembled for the purpose of collecting
evidence as to how far it is the will of
the majority of the People to acquit themselves
of this duty & exercise this right. — ~~for they~~
~~deem~~ say that purpose they ~~divide the~~

~~If the the majority of the Nation~~
~~shall be found on examination~~ ~~determine~~
~~to continue to be governed~~ be now
governed, the

This meeting shall be continued to be held
day after

9

For that purpose they divide the United
Kingdom of great Britain & Ireland into
~~to the districts equal in each of which~~
~~for this purpose they divide~~ the population
of great Britain & Ireland into 300
~~of~~ distinct portions, each to contain an
equal number ~~of persons~~ & 300 persons be
300 ~~appoints of offices~~ ~~persons~~ who might
~~be fixed for the purpose,~~ to visit personally
to visit every individual within the district
named in his commission, & to inquire whether
or no that individual is willing to sign
declaration No 2. the ~~second resolution~~, ~~with~~
requesting him to annex to his signature
any explanation he ~~might think fit~~ or
exposure of his sentiments which he might choose
to place in record. ~~That the following declaration be~~
3. That 2 that the House of Commons ~~as said~~
does not represent the People of the British
Nation; ~~or that & it is the duty of~~

the People to require that licence to originate
~~such measures as shall remedy this enormous~~
~~corruption as our reign~~ We ~~therefore declare &~~ [by unanimous] [in the face] [justice &]
declare, & our signatures annexed shall be ~~solemn~~
of our firm & solemn conviction that the
liberty, the happiness & the majesty of the
great nation to which, it is our boast to
belong, ~~are endangered are~~ [have now forced into danger & setting by degrees the] ~~Welcomes by the~~
corrupt & inadequate manner in which
~~the members of that Assembly which~~ ~~the~~
~~falsely assumes to itself the title~~ that falsely
~~call Styles~~ style themselves the representatives
~~of the nation, are~~ members are chosen to
sit in the Common House of Parliament.—
We hereby express, ~~in the~~ before God & our
Country, ~~calling~~ our deliberate & unfeigned
persuasion that it is our duty if we ~~are~~ [shall be found]
~~found~~ in the minority in this great question
[inadequately] to petition, if among the majority to require
[& to] that that House should originate such
measures of Reform, as would render its

members the actual representatives of the nation."

4. *the* That this meeting shall be held day after day, until its ~~first~~ ~~&~~ it ~~shall~~ ~~have~~ determines on the *with detail of the* ~~manner in which~~ the plan for collecting evidence as to the will of the nation on the subject of a reform in Parliament ~~shall be put in execution.~~

5 That a subscription be set on foot to defray the expenses of this plan.

In the foregoing proposal of Resolutions to be submitted to a National Meeting of the Friends of Reform, I have purposely avoided detail; ~~it being the principal feature in any~~ ~~design to excite others to a task of which~~ ~~I am no less incapable than~~ ~~frailty of weakness~~ ~~& delicacy of health, than~~ ~~feel~~ if it shall prove that I have in any degree ~~beneficial~~ ~~practically~~ ~~&~~ beneficial afforded a hint to men of ~~established~~ ~~popularity~~ who have earned & established their popularity by personal sacrifices & intellectual

eminence, ~~which~~ such [12] as I have not the presumption
to rival, it ~~belongs~~ to ~~them~~ let it belong to
them to pursue ~~the suggestions afforded by the~~
& develope ~~the cause which they~~ suggestions which
~~are the achievement of any cause~~ have ~~involuntary~~
~~presented a cause~~ all suggestions ~~which~~ ulti~~ri~~
~~to cause~~ ^a the great cause of Liberty ~~by~~ which has been nurtured (I am
scarcely conscious of a metaphor) with their very
sweat & blood & tears: Some have ^tended ~~cherished~~ ~~it~~ it in
dungeons, others have cherished it in famine
all have been constant to it amidst persecution
& calumny, & in the face of the sanctions of Power
— to accomplish what ye have begun. —

~~I~~ I shall mention ^therefore only one ~~technical~~ point ~~relating~~
to the practical part of my proposal. ^consequent Expenses
, according to my present conception, would be
~~because~~ necessarily incurred. ~~This must be mostly~~
Funds should be created by subscription to meet these
~~expense~~ demands. I have an income of
a thousand a year ^on which I ~~from~~ support my

wife & children in decent comfort & ~~from~~ ~~to~~ firm
which I satisfy certain large claims of general
justice. — Should ~~any~~ any plan resembling that
which I have proposed, be determined on by you
I will give £100 being a tenth part of one
year's income towards its object. And ~~whatever~~
~~confidently~~ I will not deem so proudly of myself
as to believe that I shall stand alone in this
~~when devotion to the public good~~ when any
~~temperate &~~ rational & consistent scheme for the
for the ~~benefit~~ ~~good~~ shall have recieved the sanction
of the ~~great~~ & good men, who have devoted
themselves for its preservation.

~~The leading features in my plan is~~
~~The only leading points~~
A certain degree of coalition among the sincere
friends of Reform in whatever shape, is indispensable to
the success of this Proposal. ~~The advocates of annual~~
~~Parliaments & Universal~~ ~~Suffrage require some~~
~~sacrifice of the object the motives~~ The friends of
Universal or of limited Suffrage, of Annual or Triennial
Parliaments ought to settle these subjects &

on which they disagree, when it is <s>certain that</s> known
whether the Nation wills <s>an the</s> that measure on
which they are all agreed. It is trivial to discuss
what species of Reform shall take place, when it
yet remains a question whether there will be any
Reform or no. — <s>nothing remains for any but</s>

Meanwhile, it <s>will be established</s> <s>I am bound</s> to
state explicitly our sentiments on this question of
Reform. — <s>I am Annual Parliaments officer</s>
It appears to me that Annual Parliaments ought
to be adopted as an immediate measure. it one
which strongly tends to preserve the liberty & happiness
of the nation, <s>by enabling men to cultivate energies</s>
<s>which have it</s> It would enable men to cultivate
those energies on which the performance of the
political duties belonging to the citizen of a free
state as the sightful guardian of its prosperity,
eventually depends. It would familiarise men <s>with</s>
liberty, by disciplining them to an habitual
acquaintance with its forms. <s>It would render known</s>
<s>above</s> Political institution is <s>an</s> undoubtedly

I have no doubt that the above is a sketch by my dear friend Shelley's own hand.

Leigh Hunt

susceptible of such improvements as no rational person
can consider as possible in the present degraded
condition to which the vital imperfections in the
existing system ~~trace~~ of government has reduced the
vast multitude of men.— The securest method of
arriving at such beneficial innovations to proceed gradually
& with caution, or in the place of that order &
freedom which the friends of reform ~~could~~ assert to
be violated now, anarchy & desposition will follow.
Annual Parliaments have my intire assent.— I
will not state those general reasonings in their favour
~~which Mr. Cobbet has placed ~~ beyond the reach
which, Mr. Cobbet & other writers have already made
familiar to the public mind.—

With respect to Universal Suffrage, ~~I consider that~~
I confess I consider its adoption in the present
unprepared state of public knowledge & feeling, a
measure fraught with peril. I think that none
but those ~~who pay~~ a register their names as
paying a certain small sum in direct taxes
ought, at present, ~~to press~~ to send members to

Parliament. The consequences of the immediate extension of the elective franchise to every male adult would be to place the ~~highest~~ power in the hands of men ~~who~~ who have been rendered brutal & torpid & ferocious by ages of slavery. It is to suppose that the qualities belonging to a demagogue are such as are sufficient ~~to~~ ~~give~~ endow a legislator. I allow Major Cartwright's arguments to be unanswerable; ~~it is the right~~ abstractedly it is the right of every human being to ~~to~~ have a share in the government. That Mr. Paine's arguments are also unanswerable; ~~& who is too enough to say that~~ he would abolish the Lords & pull down the ~~King~~, careless of all the ruin & ~~those that must ensue~~ ~~I am instructed persuaded~~ that theoretically ~~a pure republic is the~~ a pure republic may be shown by inference the most obvious & irresistible to be that system of social order the fittest to produce the happiness ~~or~~ and promote the genuine

ominion of man. It [nothing?] can less consist with
reason, or afford smaller hopes of any beneficial
issue than the plan which should abolish
the Regal & the aristocratical powers be branches
of our constitution, before the public mind, this
many generations of improvent, shall have arrived
at the maturity which can discharge these symbols
of its childhood.

The Fac-simile Manuscript
photo-lithographed and printed by
W. Griggs, *Elm House, Peckham, London, S.E.*
The letter-press printing done by
Richard Clay and Sons,
Bread Street Hill,
London, E.C.
1887

The Shelley Society

PUBLICATIONS FOR 1886—7

THE SHELLEY SOCIETY.

PUBLICATIONS FOR 1886.

1. Shelley's *Adonais :* an Elegy on the Death of John Keats. Pisa, 4to, 1821. A Type-Facsimile Reprint on hand-made Paper. Edited, with a Bibliographical Introduction, by Thomas J. Wise. (*Third Edition, Revised*). *Price* 10s. *Boards.*. [*Issued.*

2. Shelley's *Hellas, a Lyrical Drama.* London, 8vo, 1822. A Type-Facsimile Reprint on hand-made Paper; together with Shelley's *Prologue to Hellas,* and Notes by Dr. Garnett and Mary W. Shelley. Edited, with an Introduction, by Thos. J. Wise. Presented by Mr. F. S. Ellis. (*Third Edition.*) *Price* 8s. *Boards.*
[*Issued.*

3. Shelley's *Alastor, or The Spirit of Solitude; and other Poems.* London, fcap. 8vo, 1816. A Type-Facsimile Reprint on hand-made Paper, with a new Preface by Bertram Dobell. (*Second Edition, Revised.*) *Price* 6s. *Boards.* [*Issued.*

4. Shelley's *Cenci* (for the Society's performance in May), with a prologue by Dr. John Todhunter; an Introduction and Notes by Harry Buxton Forman and Alfred Forman; and a Portrait of Beatrice Cenci. Crown 8vo. *Price* 2s. 6d. *Wrappers.* [*Issued.*

5. Shelley's *Vindication of Natural Diet.* London, 12mo, 1813. A Reprint, 1882, with a Prefatory Note by H. S. Salt and W. E. A. Axon. Presented by Mr. Axon. (*Second Edition.*) [*Issued.*

6. Shelley's Review of Hogg's Novel, "Memoirs of Prince Alexy Haimatoff." Now first reprinted from *The Critical Review,* Dec. 1814, on hand-made Paper, with an Extract from Prof. Dowden's article, "Some Early Writings of Shelley" (*Contemp. Rev.*, Sept. 1884). Edited, with an Introductory Note, by Thos. J. Wise. (*Third Edition, Revised.*) Crown 8vo. *Price* 2s. 6d. *Boards.*
[*Issued.*

7. *A Memoir of Shelley,* by William Michael Rossetti, with a fresh Preface; a Portrait of Shelley; and an engraving of his Tomb. (*Second Edition,* with *Contents* and a full *Index.*) Crown 8vo. *Boards.* [*Issued.*

8. *The Shelley Library: an Essay in Bibliography.* London, 8vo, 1886. Part 1. "First Editions and their Reproductions." By H. Buxton Forman. *Wrappers.* [*Issued.*

NOTE.—Copies of Nos. 1, 2, 3, 4 and 6 can be purchased from the Society's Publishers and Agents at the prices quoted above, less the usual discount. They can also be procured through the trade in the ordinary manner. Nos. 5, 7 and 8 are not on sale. The complete set of books (8 volumes) for 1886 can, however, be obtained upon payment of the subscription (one guinea) for that year.

PUBLICATIONS FOR 1887.

The Society's Publications for 1887 will be so many of the following as the funds at their disposal enable the Committee to produce. The first three are already delivered; the succeeding four are in an advanced state, and will be sent out to Members at an early date. These seven volumes will complete the Society's first issue for the current year.

1. *The Wandering Jew,* a Poem by Percy Bysshe Shelley. Edited, with an Introduction, by Bertram Dobell. 8vo. *Price 8s. Boards.* [*Issued.*

2. *A Shelley Primer,* by Mr. H. S. Salt. This is published by Messrs. Reeves and Turner, and the Society has taken a copy for each of its Members. [*Issued.*

3. The Pianoforte Score of Dr. W. C. Selle's Choruses and Recitatives, composed for the Society's performance of Shelley's *Hellas* in November, 1886. Imperial 8vo. *Wrappers. Price 4s.* [*Issued.*

4. Shelley's *Address to the Irish People.* Dublin, 8vo, 1812. A Type-Facsimile Reprint on hand-made Paper. Edited by Thos. J. Wise. With an Introduction by T. W. Rolleston. Presented by Mr. Walter B. Slater. *Price 5s. Boards.* [*Ready Immediately.*

5. Shelley's *Necessity of Atheism.* Worthing, 12mo, (N.D. but 1811). A Type-Facsimile Reprint on hand-made Paper. Edited, with an Introduction, by Thos. J. Wise. Presented by the Editor. *Price 3s. Boards.* [*Ready Immediately.*

6. Shelley's *Masque of Anarchy.* Small 8vo, written in 1819, published in 1832. A Type-Facsimile Reprint on hand-made Paper, with full collations and fresh readings (including a hitherto unpublished stanza) from Shelley's lately discovered holograph manuscript which is now in the Editor's possession. Edited, with an Introduction, by Thomas J. Wise. *Price 5s. Boards.* [*Ready Immediately.*

7. Shelley's *Epipsychidion.* London, 8vo, 1821. A Type-Facsimile Reprint on hand-made Paper; with an Introduction by the Rev. Stopford A. Brooke, M.A., and a Note on the text of the poem by Algernon C. Swinburne. Edited by Robert A. Potts. Presented by the Editor. *Price 6s. Boards.* [*Ready Immediately.*

8. The Shelley Society's *Papers*, Part I. by the Rev. Stopford A. Brooke, M.A.; Mathilde Blind; W. M. Rossetti; H. Buxton Forman, Dr. Todhunter, &c. Part I, Nos. 1, 2, 3, and 4, are now at press.

9. The Shelley Society's *Note-Book*, Part I. Edited by the Honorary Secretary.

10. Biographical Articles on Shelley, Part I : those by Stockdale, from his *Budget* 1826–7 ; by Hogg, from *The New Monthy Magazine*, 1832–3 ; by a "Newspaper Editor," from *Fraser*, June, 1841 ; by Thornton Hunt, from *The Atlantic Monthly*, February, 1863 ; and by Peacock, from *Fraser*, 1858, 1860, and 1862. With two Portraits. Edited, with a Preface, by Thomas J. Wise. On hand-made paper. Octavo. *Price 12s. Boards.* [*Preparing.*

11. Robert Browning's *Essay and Poems on Shelley.* (Reprinted by permission of the Author.) With a Portrait of Mr. Browning, and Forewords by Dr. F. J. Furnivall. Octavo. *Boards.*
[*Preparing.*

12. *Posthumous Fragments of Margaret Nicholson.* 4to. 1810. A Type-Facsimile Reprint on hand-made Paper. Prepared from the copies of the excessively rare original in the possession of Mr. F. Locker-Lampson, and in the British Museum. Edited, with an Introduction, by Thomas J. Wise. With a Portrait of Margaret Nicholson. *Price 10s. Boards.* [*Preparing.*

13. Shelley's *Refutation of Deism.* London, 8vo, 1814. A Type-Facsimile Reprint on hand-made Paper, prepared from the excellent copy of the original in the possession of Dr. Richard Garnett. Edited by Thomas J. Wise. *Price 7s. Boards.*
[*Preparing.*

14. *A Letter to Lord Ellenborough.* Crown 8vo. (Not dated, but 1812.) A Type-Facsimile Reprint on hand-made Paper. Edited by Thomas J. Wise. Reproduced from the unique copy of the original in the possession of Sir Percy F. Shelley, Bart. *Price 5s. Boards.* [*Preparing.*

15. *Proposals for an Association of Philanthropists.* 8vo. (Not dated, but 1812.) A Type-Facsimile Reprint on hand-made Paper. Edited by Thomas J. Wise.

16. A Facsimile of Mr. H. Buxton Forman's copy of *Laon ana Cythna* as corrected by Shelley into the *Revolt of Islam.* Edited, with an Introduction, by H. Buxton Forman. [*Preparing.*

17. The Shelley Society's *Papers*, Part II, containing the chief Papers read during 1887.

18. The Shelley Society's *Note-Book*, Part II, edited by the Honorary Secretary. [Contributions of *Shelleyana* for the pages of the *Note-Book* are at all times desired.]

EXTRA SERIES.

1. The Pianoforte score of Dr. W. C. Selle's Choruses and Recitatives, composed for the Society's performance of Shelley's *Hellas* in November, 1886. Imperial 8vo. *Wrappers. Price 4s.*
[*Issued.*

2. A cheap edition of *Hellas*, prepared for the Society's performance of the drama. Edited (with a brief Introduction) by Thomas J. Wise. 8vo. *Price 3s.* in *boards* (on fine paper, with a Portrait of Shelley, one hundred copies only printed), or 2s. in wrappers. [*Issued.*

3. Shelley's *Hymn of Pan*, set to music by his son, Sir Percy F. Shelley, Bart., in 1864. This has not hitherto been publicly circulated, but *one hundred copies* have now been printed for sale for the benefit of the Society by Sir Percy's permission. Folio. Price 3s.   [*Issued.*

4. Shelley's *Masque of Anarchy*. Small 8vo, 1832. An exact reproduction by photo-lithography (by W. Griggs, of Elm House, Peckham) of the recently-discovered holograph manuscript, now in the possession of Mr. Thomas J. Wise. With an Introduction by H. Buxton Forman. 4to. *Price* 10s. *Boards.* (*Five hundred copies only* have been printed. No more will at any time be produced.)   [*Issued.*

5. Shelley's *Proposal for putting Reform to the Vote throughout the Kingdom.* 8vo. 1817. An exact reproduction by photo-lithography (by W. Griggs, of Elm House, Peckham) of the original holograph manuscript in the possession of Mr. Thomas J. Wise. With an illustration of Shelley's house at Marlow, and an Introduction by H. Buxton Forman. (A detailed account of this manuscript will be found in *The Shelley Library*, pp. 65-6.) 4to. *Price* 10s. *Boards.* (*Five Hundred copies only* have been printed. No more will at any time be produced.)   [*Issued.*

6. *Shelley at Oxford*, by Thomas Jefferson Hogg. A cheap Edition, reprinted from the Society's *Publications*, Series III., Section I, Part I. 8vo. *Wrappers. Price* 2s. 6d.   [*Preparing.*

7. *Memoirs of Shelley*, by Thomas Love Peacock: A cheap Edition, reprinted from the Society's *Publications*, Series III, Section I, Part I. 8vo. *Wrappers. Price* 2s. 6d.   [*Preparing.*

LARGE PAPER COPIES.

A few Large-Paper copies (Quarto size) of some of the Society's Publications have been privately printed ; they can be obtained upon application to Mr. Bertram Dobell, 66, Queen's Crescent, Haverstock Hill, London, N.W. The volumes now ready are :—

1. *Hellas*, with an etched frontispiece on India-paper. Fifteen copies only printed.

2. Shelley's Review of *Memoirs of Prince Alexy Haimatoff*, with an etched frontispiece on India-paper. Sixteen copies only printed.

3. *Alastor.* Fifteen copies only printed.

4. *The Wandering Jew.* Twenty-one copies only printed.

PUBLISHERS AND AGENTS.

The Society's Publishers and Agents are :—

Publishers : REEVES AND TURNER, 196, Strand, London, W.C.

Agents : CHARLES HUTT, Clement's Inn Gateway, Strand, London, W.C. ; BERTRAM DOBELL, 66, Queen's Crescent, Haverstock Hill, London, N.W.

Library Edition of Shelley.

PUBLISHED BY REEVES & TURNER, 196 STRAND.

NOW READY,

THE WHOLE WORKS

OF

PERCY BYSSHE SHELLEY

IN VERSE AND PROSE

EDITED WITH NOTES AND APPENDICES

BY

H. BUXTON FORMAN.

WITH COPIOUS INDEX OF SUBJECTS, INDEX OF FIRST LINES,
PEDIGREE, SHIELDS OF ARMS, PORTRAITS, VIEWS,
FACSIMILES, &c.

Eight Volumes, demy 8vo, Emblematically Gilt Cloth,

Contents lettered at back,

Price £5.

" . . . the typographical execution is all that the most fastidious could
desire, while it is symbolical of the critical care that has been bestowed by
the most conscientious of Editors."—*Times.*

[*See over*.

Also to be had separately, a re-issue of Mr. Buxton Forman's
Annotated Library Edition of

SHELLEY'S POETICAL WORKS,

With Mrs. SHELLEY's Notes, an Index of First Lines,
and a copious Subject Index.

Four Volumes, Demy 8vo.

With Portrait of Shelley; Etchings by Arthur Evershed of Shelley's Birth-
place, Residence at Marlow, and Grave; Etching by W. B. Scott from
Guido's Cenci; and five Facsimiles of MSS., executed by George Tupper.

**In Cloth Gilt Extra, with Emblematic Designs, and Contents lettered at
back, £2 10s.**

The principle on which Mr. Forman has prepared the text had not before
been applied to Shelley's Works. The volumes published by Shelley during
his lifetime are re-printed precisely as they stand, except where there are
obvious printer's errors, or writer's inadvertencies; but, as these are often
matters of opinion, the Editor does not deviate in so much as a comma or a
single letter from the original, without indicating in a foot-note the precise
change made. Some of the most important of those Poems which first appeared after Shelley's death are given from manuscript sources, instead of
being reproduced from the incorrect editions hitherto circulated; and for
purposes of revision, as well as for variorum readings, manuscripts of works
published in the poet's life-time, as well as those of posthumous works, have
been consulted. The highly important Leigh Hunt manuscripts, the actual
copy of *Laon and Cythna* on which Shelley made the MS. changes converting
the Poem into *The Revolt of Islam*, Shelley's own copy of *Queen Mab*, most
copiously revised, and other special sources of information, have enabled the
Editor not only to set the text right with absolute certainty in numerous
instances, but also to give the reading public Poems by Shelley not hitherto
known to Shelley students; and the first volume contains a poem on Shelley's
death by his widow. Explanatory notes are given when thought needful;
but, as the main object of the edition is to restore the text to what Shelley
wrote, the notes are generally in defence of the readings adopted, or in refutation of readings adopted elsewhere. All the copyright poems are, by special
arrangement, included.

"The revision of the text has been carried out in the most thorough manner,
and every variety of reading noted." "Mr. Forman has produced the most
complete and authentic edition of Shelley which has till now been published."
—*Saturday Review.*
"We have here an edition of Shelley's poems, which, in beauty, carefulness,
and fidelity to printed texts, is superior to any that have gone before it."—
Athenæum.
"It is superbly got up..." "Not the least valuable part of Mr. Forman's ably
executed work is the section in each volume devoted to a philological criticism of
the obsolete and rare words used by Shelley in his poems..."—*Notes and Queries.*
"It is difficult to convey any idea of the immense labour that has been devoted
to the task of clearing up corruptions in the text."—*London Quarterly Review.*
"We find in Mr. Forman's various introductions and comments the most
sagacious and sympathetic criticism."—*World.*
"Without doubt the most adequate tribute to Shelley's genius yet produced."
—*Examiner.*

Library Edition of Keats.

———————

THE

COMPLETE WORKS OF JOHN KEATS,

IN VERSE AND PROSE,

INCLUDING NUMEROUS UNPUBLISHED PIECES.

EDITED WITH NOTES AND APPENDICES

BY

H. BUXTON FORMAN.

WITH INDEXES OF SUBJECTS AND FIRST LINES,
RECOLLECTIONS OF PERSONAL FRIENDS,
PORTRAITS, VIEWS,
&c. &c.

Four Volumes, demy 8vo.

KEATS'S LETTERS.

In One Volume, Foolscap 8vo., cloth, bevelled boards,

Price 8s. 6d.,

LETTERS OF JOHN KEATS TO FANNY BRAWNE,

*Written in the years 1819 and 1820, and now first given
from the original MSS.,*

WITH INTRODUCTION, NOTES, APPENDIX, AND INDEX,

BY

H. BUXTON FORMAN,

Illustrated with SEVERN's last portrait of KEATS, etched by W. B. SCOTT; a silhouette of FANNY BRAWNE, and an exquisite fac-simile of a three-page letter, printed upon actual paper of the period.

"It is full of most important disclosures with regard to the hidden springs of Keats's life and thought. It reveals to us in a new light, not only the man, but also the poet. . . . In a certain sense, the publication of these letters might even be called the fulfilment of a duty."—*Pall Mall Gazette.*

"Nothing in the literature of this century has been so much looked forward to and desired as these love letters. . . . Mr. Forman has displayed in editing them a scrupulous care and a tasteful delicacy that will do him great credit. He is a bibliographer of genius, and on every obscure point he has patiently concentrated the light of investigation."—*Academy.*

LONDON: REEVES & TURNER, 196 STRAND.

www.ingramcontent.com/pod-product-compliance
Lightning Source LLC
Chambersburg PA
CBHW031440270326
41930CB00007B/795